THE AMAZING HUMAN BODY

THE HUMAN
NERVOUS SYSTEM

by Chelsea Xie

BrightPoint Press

San Diego, CA

© 2025 BrightPoint Press
an imprint of ReferencePoint Press, Inc.
Printed in the United States

For more information, contact:
BrightPoint Press
PO Box 27779
San Diego, CA 92198
www.BrightPointPress.com

ALL RIGHTS RESERVED.
No part of this work covered by the copyright hereon may be reproduced or used in any form or by any means—graphic, electronic, or mechanical, including photocopying, recording, taping, web distribution, or information storage retrieval systems—without the written permission of the publisher.

LIBRARY OF CONGRESS CATALOGING-IN-PUBLICATION DATA

Name: Xie, Chelsea, author.
Title: The human nervous system / by Chelsea Xie.
Description: San Diego, CA: BrightPoint Press, 2025 | Series: The amazing human body | Audience: Grade 7 to 9 | Includes bibliographical references and index.
Identifiers: ISBN: 9781678209667 (hardcover) | ISBN: 9781678209674 (eBook)
The complete Library of Congress record is available at www.loc.gov.

CONTENTS

AT A GLANCE   4

INTRODUCTION   6
   CARING FOR JACQUELYN

CHAPTER ONE   12
   WHAT IS THE NERVOUS SYSTEM?

CHAPTER TWO   24
   HOW DOES THE NERVOUS SYSTEM WORK?

CHAPTER THREE   34
   WHAT CAN GO WRONG WITH THE NERVOUS SYSTEM?

CHAPTER FOUR   48
   WHAT CAN HUMANS DO TO KEEP THE NERVOUS SYSTEM HEALTHY?

Glossary	58
Source Notes	59
For Further Research	60
Index	62
Image Credits	63
About the Author	64

AT A GLANCE

- The nervous system is the command center of the body. It communicates with other body systems using electrical and chemical signals.

- The nervous system has many roles. It allows for sensation, movement, thought, memory, and more.

- The nervous system is mostly made up of nerve cells called neurons.

- The nervous system can be divided into the central nervous system (CNS) and the peripheral nervous system (PNS).

- Many disorders can affect the nervous system. These include epilepsy, dementia, and multiple sclerosis (MS).

- Some diseases can affect the nervous system. Medical events can affect the nervous system, too.

- There are ways to keep the nervous system healthy. Eating a well-balanced diet, getting regular exercise, and having healthy sleep habits all help the nervous system.

- Mental exercises can have long-term benefits for the nervous system. These exercises include solving word puzzles and learning new languages.

INTRODUCTION

CARING FOR JACQUELYN

Laury sat in the nursing home with her mother. Her mother's name was Jacquelyn. Jacquelyn was only 60 years old. She was much younger than most of the other residents. But Jacquelyn was having problems caring for herself. She forgot to eat and shower. Her neighbors sometimes found her wandering around. She would be completely lost.

Besides its effects on memory, Alzheimer's disease can also impair a person's movement.

Nursing homes are facilities where people who need daily care can live.

Jacquelyn was in her fifties when she was **diagnosed** with Alzheimer's disease. This disease affects memory. It also causes problems with making decisions.

Jacquelyn walked around the halls of the nursing home. Laury followed close behind. She thought about her mom's condition.

Small changes helped Jacquelyn at first. Sticky notes served as helpful reminders. Her mother began taking the bus instead of driving. This meant she no longer had to remember where she had parked.

But now Jacquelyn was in the later stages of the disease. Laury realized that the disease was more than forgetfulness. Sometimes her mother didn't recognize her.

Jacquelyn turned around. She smiled at Laury and took her hand. Laury wasn't sure if her mother knew that she was her daughter. But she was grateful that Jacquelyn still felt safe around her.

THE NERVOUS SYSTEM

Alzheimer's disease affects the nervous system. This body system includes the brain

The nervous system allows people to make precise, deliberate movements, such as writing by hand.

and spinal cord. It also includes the nerves. Nerves are made up of cells called neurons.

The nervous system helps people respond to their surroundings. It controls movement. It allows people to think and learn. It also oversees emotion and memory.

Some diseases and injuries affect the nervous system. This can have a big impact on people's lives. Some diseases do not have cures. These include Alzheimer's. But there are ways to treat or **adapt** to many diseases. And people can take steps to keep the nervous system healthy. This can reduce the risk of getting some diseases.

CHAPTER ONE

WHAT IS THE NERVOUS SYSTEM?

The nervous system controls all other body systems. It does this by sending electrical and chemical signals. The nervous system receives information from outside and within the body. It processes this information. Then it sends signals. The signals cause the body to react.

Sensing is a major role of the nervous system. Humans have five main senses.

A sense called proprioception allows people to know where their body parts are without having to look at them.

The retina is the part in the back of the eye that contains sensory neurons. These neurons send signals to the brain through the optic nerve.

They are sight, hearing, taste, smell, and touch. Other senses include balance.

Sensing is possible thanks to sensory neurons. These cells take in information from the world. For example, the back of the eye contains sensory neurons. Light strikes these neurons. Then the neurons fire. This means they send electrical signals to the brain. The brain turns these signals into images.

Some sensory neurons respond to injury. Pain nerves near the site of the injury send signals to the brain. The brain triggers a response. This produces feelings of pain.

Life without pain might sound great. But pain is important. Dr. Leonard Kamen works in pain management. "You need pain," he says. "It's part of our defense network that helps protect us from injury and threat."[1] Pain alerts the body to danger. This can prevent further injury. For example, pain allows a person to know that a sharp object is underfoot. It stops the person from putting more weight on the foot.

MOVEMENT

Muscles allow the body to move. But it is the nervous system that causes movement. It does this by sending signals through special neurons called motor neurons.

Motor neurons link the brain and spinal cord with other body parts. These include **glands**, organs, and muscles.

Body movement is divided into two types. Actions that people can control are one type. These include moving the limbs. The second type includes movements that people do not have to think about. Digestion is an example of this kind

A Body in Balance

The nervous system keeps functions inside of the body stable. For example, the nervous system keeps the body at a nearly constant temperature. It uses shivering and sweating to do this. A stable body temperature is important. The body's organs work best at temperatures around 98.6°F (37°C). The nervous system also helps regulate other things. These include blood sugar and oxygen levels.

The nervous system typically makes breathing happen automatically. But people can also control their breathing.

of movement. Digestion is how the body absorbs nutrients from food. Muscles push food through the stomach and intestines. People do not control these muscles. The nervous system moves them on its own.

THINKING, LEARNING, AND FEELING

The nervous system produces mental processes. These include thinking and learning. They also include feeling emotions. Neurons in the brain make these processes possible.

Scientists are still studying how neurons produce mental processes. Communication among neurons may be responsible. The brain is made up of about 100 billion neurons. One neuron can be connected to

When people practice the same motion several times, they can learn to make the motion without having to focus on it. This helps people smoothly perform some skills, such as playing instruments.

more than 1,000 other neurons. Professor Lina Begdache says,

> "One theory explains that thoughts are [created] when neurons fire. Our external environment . . . leads to a pattern of neuron firing, which results in a thought process."[2]

Learning may occur as groups of neurons fire together over time. For example, a person might learn to play the guitar. A group of neurons fires whenever they play a guitar. The connections between the neurons become stronger with practice. This allows the person to improve their skill over time.

Emotions also occur when groups of neurons fire. Researchers have identified several areas of the brain that play a role in emotion. The amygdala is one such area.

Sensory memories, such as memories of touching the rough surface of sandpaper, only last for up to a few seconds.

This part helps people recall emotional memories. It also plays a role in fear.

MEMORY

The nervous system creates and stores memories. Many areas of the brain are involved in memory. Different types of memories activate different brain regions.

There are several ways researchers think about memory. Some research describes sensory memory. This type of memory is very short-lived. It involves memories of sensory experiences. Sensory memory helps people understand what they are seeing. It helps people follow conversations.

Short-term memory is another type of memory. Short-term memory is sometimes called working memory. A short-term memory lasts for about 30 seconds. People can work to keep short-term memories in mind. For example, a person might repeat a phone number in her head. This helps her remember it before she can write it down. The front part of the brain oversees short-term memory.

Memories that last for longer than a few minutes are long-term memories. Long-term memory allows people to recall motor skills. People do not need to relearn how to type each time they sit in front of a computer. A part of the brain called the cerebellum helps people remember motor skills.

Long-term memory also helps people remember facts. It is at work when a person thinks about who won the last Super Bowl. It allows students to answer questions

Memories of life events are called episodic memories.

on a test. Long-term memory is key to remembering life events. A person may have a memory of the first time he went camping. Scoring the winning goal of a soccer game can be a long-term memory. Neurons throughout the brain help with memorizing facts and life events.

CHAPTER TWO

HOW DOES THE NERVOUS SYSTEM WORK?

Neurons are the building blocks of the nervous system. These cells make up the brain and spinal cord. They also make up nerves. These fibers extend throughout the body.

Neurons vary in shape and size. But all share some common parts. A neuron has dendrites. These structures receive signals from other neurons. Signals then travel to the cell body of the neuron. The cell

The longest nerve in the human body is the sciatic nerve. It runs from the lower back to the foot and allows for movements such as squatting.

body provides energy for the neuron. Then signals travel along the axon. The axon is a long branch that extends from the cell body. The axon sends signals to the dendrites of other neurons.

A layer of fatty protein coats the axon. This layer is called the myelin sheath. It allows signals to travel quickly along the axon. There are tiny gaps in the sheath. Electrical signals jump from gap to gap. This is faster than traveling through the

Glial Cells

Neurons are not the only cells that make up the nervous system. Glial cells are also part of this body system. These cells provide support to neurons. They help protect the brain from dangerous chemicals. They also help produce the myelin sheath.

entire axon. Myelin sheaths develop over time after birth. Dr. Colleen Doherty says, "If you've ever noticed the jerky, sudden movements babies make, this is because their myelin sheaths aren't fully developed at birth."[3]

Neurons are not physically connected. Small gaps called synapses separate neurons. Electrical signals typically do not cross these gaps. Instead, one neuron's axon releases chemical messengers. These chemicals bind to the dendrites of the other neuron. This causes the neuron to create its own electrical signal. This process continues from neuron to neuron.

Three kinds of neurons make up the nervous system. Sensory and motor neurons are the first two. Interneurons are the third. These neurons link sensory and motor neurons. Interneurons are found only in the brain and spinal cord. They are the most common kind of neuron in the body.

CENTRAL NERVOUS SYSTEM

The nervous system can be divided into two main sections. The central nervous system (CNS) is one section. It includes the brain and spinal cord. Each region of the brain has unique jobs. The brain has three main parts. They are the brain stem, cerebellum, and cerebrum.

The brain stem rests at the base of the brain. It connects the brain to the spinal cord. The brain stem controls processes such as breathing and heart rate. It also plays a role in balance.

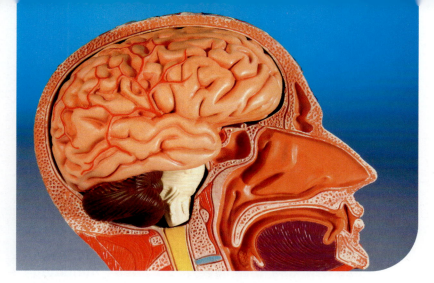

Although the brain makes up only 2 percent of the body's weight, it uses 20 percent of the body's energy.

The cerebellum is at the back of the brain. It holds more than half of the brain's neurons. This part of the brain helps coordinate movement. It may also play a role in understanding language.

The cerebrum makes up about 80 percent of the brain. It is divided into halves. The right half controls the left side of the body. The left half controls the right side of the body.

The cerebrum has many jobs. It takes in information from the senses. It helps people

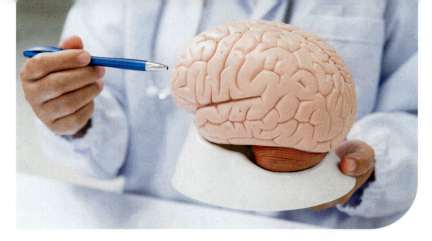

The surface of the cerebrum is wrinkled. Scientists think these wrinkles have several purposes, including increasing the brain's surface area. This allows the brain to fit more neurons into the skull.

talk and solve problems. It plays a role in memory. This part also controls emotions and behavior.

The spinal cord is the second part of the CNS. It is a thick bundle of nerves. It runs through the spine. This cord connects the brain to nerves throughout the body.

The spinal cord has three main functions. It sends sensory information to the brain. It relays motor commands from the brain to the body. It also oversees reflexes. Reflexes are actions that occur automatically.

The spinal cord controls reflexes on its own. No input from the brain is necessary.

Reflexes allow the body to quickly respond to danger. Pulling one's hand away from a hot stove is an example of a reflex. The movement occurs before one even feels pain. Sensory neurons in the hand pick up information about the heat. They send signals to the spinal cord. The spinal cord then sends a response to motor neurons to pull the hand away.

Doctors sometimes test patients' reflexes. Problems with a reflex can be a sign of disease. "That includes the muscle, the nerve, . . . and the spinal cord, but also disease of the brain," says Dr. Eric Strong.[4]

Bones protect the brain and spinal cord. The skull surrounds the brain. The spine

One of the most commonly tested reflexes is the knee-jerk reflex.

surrounds the spinal cord. Thin layers of tissue also protect these parts. These layers wrap around the brain and spinal cord. They keep these parts in place. They also help supply them with blood.

PERIPHERAL NERVOUS SYSTEM

The peripheral nervous system (PNS) is the other section of the nervous system. It includes all nerves in the body beyond the CNS. The PNS includes twelve pairs of cranial nerves. These nerves extend from the brain. It also includes thirty-one pairs of spinal nerves. These begin at the spinal cord. Both types of nerves branch into smaller nerves. They connect to muscles and organs.

The PNS sends information to the CNS. This includes sensory information. The system also carries out commands from the brain and spinal cord. This results in actions such as movement.

CHAPTER THREE

WHAT CAN GO WRONG WITH THE NERVOUS SYSTEM?

Other body systems rely on the nervous system to function. Issues with the nervous system can be life-threatening. But many people with **chronic** nervous system conditions live full lives.

Epilepsy is a common disorder that affects the nervous system. It is often diagnosed in children and in people more than 65 years old. About 1 percent of US adults have this disorder.

One way doctors test for epilepsy is by using a device that measures the brain's electrical activity.

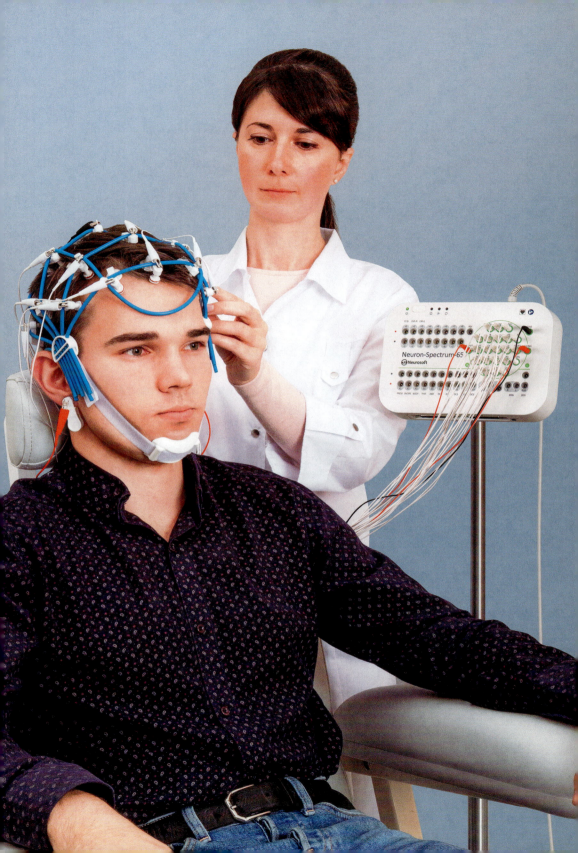

Seizures are the main symptom of epilepsy. A seizure is a surge of abnormal electrical activity in the brain. This can cause other symptoms. A seizure may cause convulsions. These are sudden movements caused by strong muscle spasms. A person having a seizure may fall

Some seizures can be life-threatening and require immediate medical attention.

to the ground. They may stare blankly into space. A seizure can also cause confusion. Many people who have seizures report sensing something that was not real. They might hear something that no one around them hears.

Epilepsy can have several different causes. These include traits inherited from one's parents. They also include injuries to the head. Infections can also cause this disorder. So can brain tumors. The cause of epilepsy is unknown in about half of people with the condition.

People can take steps to manage epilepsy. Medication can greatly reduce the risk of seizures. But it can take time to figure out the correct **dosage**. People can take additional steps to avoid seizures.

Stress and lack of sleep can increase the risk of seizures.

Epilepsy is a lifelong condition for some people. But this is not always true for children with epilepsy. Dr. Deborah Holder treats epilepsy. She explains, "As the brain grows and develops, many children will outgrow seizures."[5]

MULTIPLE SCLEROSIS

Multiple sclerosis (MS) is a disease that affects the CNS. It is an **autoimmune** disease. MS causes the body to attack the myelin sheath around neurons.

The symptoms of MS vary. People with MS may experience weakness on one side of their body. They may have balance issues. They may lose the ability to walk.

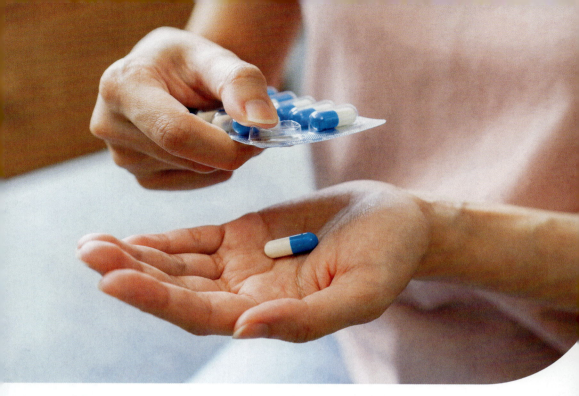

There is no cure for MS, but treatments can help control the disease's symptoms.

Some people develop vision problems. Many people with MS have symptoms that come and go. The disease can also be progressive. This means that loss of function continues over time.

DEMENTIA

Dementia describes a group of diseases. These diseases affect thinking and memory.

Other diseases that can cause dementia include Parkinson's disease and Huntington's disease.

Alzheimer's is the most common form of these diseases. It accounts for more than 60 percent of cases.

Dementia can cause forgetfulness and confusion. People with dementia may have trouble making decisions. They may struggle to follow conversations. The condition can also cause changes in behavior. People may become easily angered or frustrated. They may withdraw from social activities.

Dementia is not a normal part of aging. But age is the biggest risk factor for developing these diseases. Approximately 10 percent of adults older than 65 have some form of dementia.

Damage to neurons in the brain causes dementia. The pathways between neurons weaken. The type of damage determines the form of dementia. Alzheimer's results from a buildup of proteins in the brain. This kills nerve cells. The brain shrinks.

People lose abilities as dementia progresses. This can be frustrating. Dementia can also be challenging for friends and family members. They may need to take on a caregiving role. Dr. James

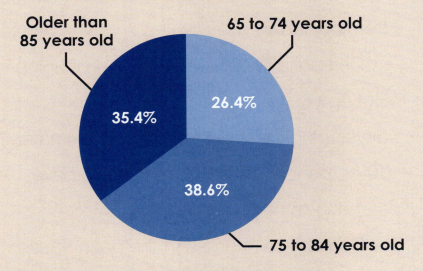

In 2024, most people with Alzheimer's dementia were more than 65 years old. Only about 0.11 percent of US adults between the ages of 30 and 65 are believed to have early-onset dementia.

Noble is a **neurologist**. He gives advice for those caring for someone with dementia. "Be patient, be supportive, and look for answers and provide them when you have them," he says.[6]

STROKES

A stroke occurs when blood flow to the brain is interrupted. This can occur in two ways. A blood vessel to the brain may become blocked. Or the vessel may burst. This causes bleeding in the brain. In both cases, the lack of blood flow results in the death of brain cells. Blood delivers oxygen to the brain. Neurons cannot survive without oxygen.

Strokes can be deadly. They are the second-most common cause of death worldwide. People of any age can have a stroke. But strokes are most common in older adults.

Responding quickly to a stroke is important. This reduces the risk of brain damage and death. Many signs can

Stroke patients need immediate medical care. Sometimes this care begins in an ambulance.

indicate that someone is having a stroke. A stroke can cause issues with balance. Sudden changes in vision are another sign. A person having a stroke may have slurred speech. A stroke often causes weakness on one side of the body. People having a stroke may have a smile that droops on one side. They may have difficulty raising one of their arms.

SPINAL CORD INJURIES

Injuries to nerves affect the nervous system. Damaged nerves have reduced function. This can cause sensory issues and movement problems.

Spinal cord injuries (SCIs) can be especially severe. They make it difficult for signals to pass through the spine. Many nerves branch out from the spinal cord. Body parts below the point of injury are affected.

About 18,000 new SCIs occur in the United States each year. These injuries can happen as a result of **trauma**. But there are many other causes. Cancer can cause an SCI. Diseases can affect blood flow to the spinal cord. This can also lead to an SCI.

Mobility devices such as wheelchairs can improve quality of life for people with SCIs.

SCIs cause a range of symptoms. They can cause numbness below the site of injury. They can also cause issues with movement. These include paralysis. This means a person may be unable to move or feel parts of their body. Many people with an SCI have muscle spasms. SCIs can cause people to lose control of other motor functions. For example, they may have trouble breathing.

SCIs can be complete or incomplete. A complete injury means there is no nerve communication below the injury site. An incomplete injury means that some signals can pass through. A person may still have some feeling below the injury site. Someone who is paralyzed may still have some control over affected limbs.

Cerebral Palsy

Cerebral palsy is a group of disorders that affect movement and posture. Symptoms can vary greatly. Common symptoms include stiff muscles and poor coordination. Many people with cerebral palsy are born with it. Signs of the disorder typically appear in infancy or early childhood. Cerebral palsy is the leading cause of disability in children.

CHAPTER FOUR

WHAT CAN HUMANS DO TO KEEP THE NERVOUS SYSTEM HEALTHY?

A healthy nervous system is key for a healthy life. The system plays a role in everything people do. Nervous system conditions can have a huge impact on life. But there are ways to keep the nervous system healthy.

A healthy diet supports neurons. To work properly, nerves require lots of nutrients. Doctors recommend eating a variety of foods. For many people, this may include

Doctors recommend that people plan healthy meals in advance instead of waiting until the meal to choose what to eat.

The US government recommends that people between ages 6 and 17 years old get at least 60 minutes of exercise every day.

whole grains, vegetables, and healthy sources of protein. A balanced diet can promote nervous system health.

Some nutrients have a strong connection to the nervous system. Minerals such as calcium help produce electrical signals. Dairy products are good sources of calcium. Foods rich in vitamin B also support nerve health. Vitamin B helps maintain the myelin sheath. This nutrient is in foods such as eggs and fish.

EXERCISE AND REDUCING STRESS

Regular exercise benefits the nervous system. Exercise helps the body repair neurons and grow new ones. It helps attention and memory, too. Exercise also improves blood flow to the brain. This can reduce the risk of some forms of dementia.

Exercise reduces stress. High levels of stress can harm the nervous system. Other activities can also reduce stress. One such activity is practicing mindfulness. This involves focusing on the present. People can practice mindfulness by paying attention to their senses or their breathing.

Getting Healthy Sleep

Healthy sleep habits can help people feel well rested in the morning. Adults should aim to get at least 7 hours of sleep each night. Teens need between 9 and 10 hours. Keeping the bedroom cool, dark, and quiet improves sleep quality. Setting a bedtime and wake-up time is a good sleep habit. Screen time should be limited before going to sleep.

Sleep can also reduce stress. Sleep refreshes the nervous system. The body removes waste from the nervous system during sleep. Sleep also improves learning. New pathways between neurons form during sleep.

People who do not get enough sleep might have trouble paying attention. They may have memory issues. Poor sleep raises the risk of some mental health disorders. It is also linked to a higher risk of Alzheimer's.

MENTAL EXERCISE

The brain needs exercise just like the rest of the body. Solving puzzles strengthens the brain. So does learning new languages. These mental exercises cause new neural pathways to form. Mental exercise also improves existing connections.

Completing puzzles improves people's problem-solving skills. Studies have also shown that puzzles boost working memory. A 2017 study looked at the effect of word puzzles. It revealed a possible connection between solving word puzzles and having strong attention and memory abilities. Further research may reveal whether puzzles can reduce the risk of dementia.

Creativity forces the brain to make new pathways. Susan Magsamen is the director of the International Arts and Mind Lab. She talks about how playing musical instruments affects children. She says, "Their brain structure actually changes and their [cerebrum] actually gets larger."[7]

Regularly solving crossword puzzles may slightly reduce brain shrinkage in older adults with mild memory or thinking impairment.

School music programs are where many young people start playing musical instruments.

Other art forms also cause these changes. These forms include dance and poetry.

The nervous system performs many tasks. It makes thinking and moving possible. It also controls automatic processes such as digestion. But things can go wrong with the nervous system. That is why it is important to take care of the nervous system. Keeping the nervous system in good shape helps people live long, healthy lives.

GLOSSARY

adapt

to adjust to new conditions

autoimmune

relating to a disease in which the body attacks itself

chronic

continuing or occurring again and again over a long period of time

diagnosed

recognized by a medical professional as having a disease or condition

dosage

the amount of medication and the frequency at which a medication is taken

glands

body parts that release substances such as saliva

neurologist

a medical doctor who diagnoses and treats disorders of the nervous system

trauma

serious physical injury to the body

SOURCE NOTES

CHAPTER ONE: WHAT IS THE NERVOUS SYSTEM?

1. Quoted in Lisa Ellis, "Why We Feel Pain and Why It Can Last So Long," *Jefferson Health*, June 6, 2022. www.jeffersonhealth.org.

2. Lina Begdache, "Ask a Scientist: Neurons Help Explain How Our Brains Think," *Press Connects*, March 17, 2019. www.pressconnects.com.

CHAPTER TWO: HOW DOES THE NERVOUS SYSTEM WORK?

3. Colleen Doherty, MD, "Myelin Sheath Function and Purpose," *Verywell Health*, June 24, 2024. www.verywellhealth.com.

4. Quoted in "Deep Tendon Reflexes – A Definitive Guide," *YouTube*, uploaded by Strong Medicine, November 18, 2020. www.youtube.com.

CHAPTER THREE: WHAT CAN GO WRONG WITH THE NERVOUS SYSTEM?

5. Quoted in "Q&A with Cedars-Sinai Guerin Children's Deborah Holder, MD," *Cedars-Sinai*, November 6, 2023. www.cedars-sinai.org.

6. Quoted in "How to Support a Loved One with Alzheimer's — and the Best Ways to Connect," *Health Matters* (blog), *NewYork-Presbyterian*, November 29, 2023. https://healthmatters.nyp.org.

CHAPTER FOUR: WHAT CAN HUMANS DO TO KEEP THE NERVOUS SYSTEM HEALTHY?

7. Quoted in Jon Hamilton, "Building a Better Brain Through Music, Dance, and Poetry," *NPR*, April 3, 2023. www.npr.org.

FOR FURTHER RESEARCH

BOOKS

Linda Cernak, *The Human Body Encyclopedia*. North Mankato, MN: Abdo Reference, 2023.

Jonas Edwards, *The Nervous System*. New York: Gareth Stevens, 2022.

Natalie Hyde, *Investigating the Nervous System*. New York: Crabtree, 2023.

INTERNET SOURCES

"How Your Brain Works," *Mayo Clinic*, July 2, 2024. www.mayoclinic.org.

"Overview of Nervous System Disorders," *Johns Hopkins Medicine*, n.d. www.hopkinsmedicine.org.

Carla Vandergriendt and Rachael Zimlich, "An Easy Guide to Neuron Anatomy with Diagrams," *Healthline*, February 28, 2022. www.healthline.com.

WEBSITES

Alzheimer's Association
www.alz.org

The Alzheimer's Association strives for an end to Alzheimer's. Its website provides information about the disease and offers support to people with Alzheimer's and their caregivers.

Cleveland Clinic
https://my.clevelandclinic.org

Cleveland Clinic is a medical center. It connects patients with medical providers. It also publishes health information, such as articles about the nervous system, for the public.

Epilepsy Foundation
www.epilepsy.com

The Epilepsy Foundation raises public awareness of epilepsy. It helps people understand what epilepsy is and gives tips to those living with the disorder.

INDEX

Alzheimer's disease, 6–11, 40–42, 53
amygdala, 21
axons, 26–27

body temperature, 16
bones, 31–32
brain stem, 28

cell body, 24–26
central nervous system (CNS), 28–33, 38
cerebellum, 22, 28–29
cerebral palsy, 47
cerebrum, 28–30, 57

dementia, 39–42, 52, 54
dendrites, 24–27
digestion, 16–18, 57

emotion, 11, 18, 20–21, 30
epilepsy, 34–38

glial cells, 26

healthy diet, 48–51

interneurons, 27–28

learning, 11, 18–20, 22, 53–54

memory, 8–11, 21–23, 30, 39, 51, 53–54
mental exercise, 53–57
motor neurons, 15–16, 27–28, 31
movement, 11, 15–18, 27, 29, 31, 33, 36, 45–47, 57
multiple sclerosis (MS), 38–39
myelin sheath, 26–27, 38, 51

nutrients, 18, 48–51

pain, 14–15, 31
peripheral nervous system (PNS), 33
physical exercise, 51–52

reflexes, 30–31

sensing, 12–15, 21, 29–31, 33, 37, 45, 53
sensory neurons, 14–15, 27–28, 31
sleep, 38, 52–53
spinal cord, 9, 16, 24, 28, 30–33, 45–47
spinal cord injuries (SCIs), 45–47
stress, 38, 52–53
strokes, 43–44
synapses, 27

IMAGE CREDITS

Cover: © Prostock-Studio/Shutterstock Images
5: © New Africa/Shutterstock Images
7: © Amorn Suriyan/Shutterstock Images
8: © Robert Kneschke/Shutterstock Images
10: © fizkes/Shutterstock Images
13: © Miljan Zivkovic/Shutterstock Images
14: © NagyDodo/Shutterstock Images
17: © Pheelings Media/Shutterstock Images
19: © SeventyFour/Shutterstock Images
20: © New Africa/Shutterstock Images
23: © matimix/Shutterstock Images
25: © Nikita Sursin/Shutterstock Images
29: © Steve Allen/Shutterstock Images
30: © Komsan Loonprom/Shutterstock Images
32: © Lordn/Shutterstock Images
35: © Alexandra_Skor/Shutterstock Images
36: © Gioele Piccinini/Shutterstock Images
39: © Kmpzzz/Shutterstock Images
40: © Inside Creative House/Shutterstock Images
42: © Red Line Editorial
44: © Ceri Breeze/Shutterstock Images
46: © LightField Studios/Shutterstock Images
49: © s_oleg/Shutterstock Images
50: © milatas/Shutterstock Images
55: © Dmitriy Prayzel/Shutterstock Images
56: © Daisy Daisy/Shutterstock Images

ABOUT THE AUTHOR

Chelsea Xie lives in San Diego, California. She solves crossword puzzles and swims to keep her mind and body healthy.